This Book Belongs To:

____

"Jasper in Jasper"
A True Canadian Tail

First Edition

ISBN: 978-1-0690151-0-5

Copyright © 2024 by Amanda Skwarok

This book is a work of non-fiction. Names, characters, places, and incidents are factual, and every effort has been made to ensure that the information provided is accurate and current as of the date of publication. However, the author and publisher assume no responsibility for errors, omissions, or contrary interpretation of the subject matter herein. For permissions or licensing inquiries, please contact the author directly.

A Heartfelt Thank You

To the wonderful town of Jasper, thank you for
your incredible support and kindness during our
search. Your community spirit made all the difference.

To my incredible parents, thank you for your unwavering
love, help, and encouragement. Your hope and strength
kept us all going during the difficult days of the rescue.

To my Jasper bear, thank you for the cherished memories
and the unbreakable bond we shared. This story is a
testament to our adventures together and to
a love and connection that will never fade.

With gratitude,
Amanda Skwarok

~

JASPER and his owner, Amanda, were on their way to Jasper National Park for a Canada Day camping trip. Jasper's tail wagged with excitement as he looked out the window at the passing scenery. He loved car rides, especially when they meant new adventures in the mountains together.

Amanda smiled at Jasper. "I named you after this special mountain town because of all the wonderful memories I have here with my family. We've made some great ones of our own too!" Jasper gave a happy bark, as if to say, "I know! I can't wait to make more this weekend!"

When they arrived at their favourite spot,
Whistlers Campground, the sign showed it was full.
"Don't worry, Jasper, there are plenty of great
campsites here!" Amanda said reassuringly.
They found a sight at Kerkeslin Campground
and soon fell asleep under the starlit sky.

Whistlers
Jasper National Park
Parc national Jasper
Full/Complet

The next morning, they woke up to the familiar caws of the ravens. Amanda, eager to start the day, greeted Jasper cheerfully, "Good morning! Ready for some Canada Day adventures?"
She tied a bright red bandana around his neck. "You look great, Jasper! Let's go!"

Their first stop was Horseshoe Lake. Jasper was bursting with energy and ran through the bushes as fast as he could. Amanda chuckled, watching him enjoy the zoomies. "You sure love being in the mountains, don't you, Jasper?"

Amanda captured a photo of Jasper before they left Horseshoe Lake. "You've had so much fun today, running around and showing off your new bandana. This picture will be a great memory of our trip!" Jasper shook off the zoomies and barked happily, eager for more adventures.

As evening approached, they made their way to Centennial Park for the Canada Day celebrations. The park was filled with locals and tourists enjoying the festivities. They found a cozy spot to watch the fireworks and shared a tasty snow cone. "How's the treat, Jasper? Looks like it's melting faster than you can eat it!" Amanda laughed.

Suddenly, the fireworks started with a loud BOOM! Jasper's ears perked up, and he looked worried. "It's okay, Jasper! It's just fireworks," Amanda reassured him, but Jasper was frightened. He broke free from his collar and bolted into the crowd! "Jasper, come back!" Amanda cried out.

Scared and confused, Jasper slipped under the fence that surrounds the park. He raced past the town, crossing the bridge above the Miette River, the road that connects the town to the wilderness. The loud noises slowly faded, but fear kept Jasper running all the way to Whistlers Campground.

Drawn by the familiar scent of campfire smoke, Jasper's hopes lifted. "Maybe I can find our campsite!" he thought. Jasper searched for hours, unaware that he was in the wrong campground... Eventually, he got tired and found an empty fox den by the river to rest in for the night.

Meanwhile, back in town, Amanda was searching

frantically, shouting, "Jasper, where are you?!"

She ran past a group of people, one chuckled

and pointed at a sign. "You're in Jasper, silly."

Amanda's face turned red with frustration.

"I know! I'm looking for my dog named JASPER!"

Exhausted from searching on foot, Amanda drove around town, calling out the window for her dog. "Jasper, where are you?" she pleaded. After hours of looking for him with no luck, she returned to the campsite at Kerkeslin, hoping someone had found her pup and was keeping him safe.

As soon as the sun came up, Amanda rushed into town to make lost dog posters. She used the most recent photo of Jasper at Horseshoe Lake. "That red bandana will help others find you, I won't give up, Jasper," she declared, as she put up the posters around town.

Moments later, Amanda's phone buzzed with reports of Jasper spotted on Whistlers Mountain. "I'm coming!" she shouted, setting off to find him. She hiked all day, but he was still nowhere to be found. As the sun began to set, they were both left to face another lonely night apart.

The next day, Jasper was hungry and went searching for food. He climbed halfway up Whistlers Mountain and found a bush with ripe berries. Suddenly, a big black bear roared, "Arrr, these are my berries! You've eaten nearly all of them. Maybe I should eat you for a snack!" Terrified, Jasper bolted up the mountain.

Tired and thirsty, Jasper was relieved to find an icy cool stream. Suddenly, two wolves appeared. "This stream isn't for you; it's for us bigger animals. You're no bigger than the rabbits we hunt, "growled the first wolf. "He looks like a tasty rabbit to me!" snarled the second wolf. Frightened once again, Jasper quickly bolted down the mountain.

Meanwhile, at Kerkeslin, Amanda packed up her belongings. A spot had opened up at Whistlers Campground. "Now I will be closer to Jasper!" Amanda exclaimed. Upon arrival, she followed the advice of the campground workers and hung up her clothes along with Jasper's items, hoping the familiar scents would help him find her.

With her new campsite set up, Amanda made urgent phone calls seeking help in the search and rescue efforts. Her first call was to her parents. After hearing the upsetting news, they quickly packed their camping gear and made their way to the mountains to help find Jasper.

Next, Amanda contacted the Information Centre
in the town of Jasper. Moved by the lost dog story,
the workers organized two volunteer search teams
to cover the areas where Jasper had been spotted.
Soon, everyone in Jasper was looking for JASPER.

Amanda also called the Warden's Station for assistance. Moments later, a kind park ranger arrived with a fox trap. "Set the trap along the Miette River, where he has been spotted most. Place some wet dog food inside and be careful not to catch any other animals," advised the ranger.

After placing the trap, Amanda and her parents split up to search Whistlers Mountain. But Amanda soon returned after encountering the two wolves, and her mom hurried back after spotting the big black bear. Luckily, her dad only came across a harmless deer, but there was still no sign of Jasper. Then, it began to rain...

While everyone searched for Jasper, he spent the day sleeping in the empty fox den. Suddenly, he heard a noise. "Hello? Who's there?" he barked. The harmless deer appeared and reassured him, "Don't be afraid, little one. Your family is looking for you. They've left a trap with food in it further up the river. You should take a look."

Trusting the deer, Jasper ventured out of the den, but the rain grew stronger, washing away most of the food before he reached the trap. As he got closer, the sound of the raindrops hitting the trap spooked him, and he ran away. "I guess I'll try again tomorrow," he whimpered.

The heavy rain continued into the next day.
It had been a week now since Jasper ran away and
messages about his sightings were becoming less
frequent. "Please, let this be the day we find him,"
Amanda sighed as she checked the trap early in
the morning, but the trap was still empty...

Later that morning, Amanda and her dad drove to check the trap while her mom stayed behind to make brunch. Feeling sad and nervous, Amanda stayed in the vehicle, hoping her dad would return with good news.

When Amanda saw her dad without Jasper, her heart began to drop. He walked over to her window, tears welling in his eyes. With a mix of hope and fear, she slowly opened the door. "Amanda, we got him! JASPER is inside the trap!" he cheered. Her face lit up with joy and disbelief. "Really? I can't believe it!" she exclaimed.

They brought Jasper back to the campsite and opened up the trap. He leaped out and gave Amanda a big, wet kiss. "I missed you so much!" she cried, hugging him tightly. "We're so glad he's safe. We couldn't have done this without the community's support, or without each other," her mom said gratefully.

JASPER
fitzHUGH

Jasper's celebrated return was featured in the local Jasper Fitzhugh newspaper later that month.
Not all dogs are as lucky to survive a week in the Canadian Rockies. Jasper and Amanda continued to visit Jasper National Park for many years after the rescue, creating wonderful new memories together.

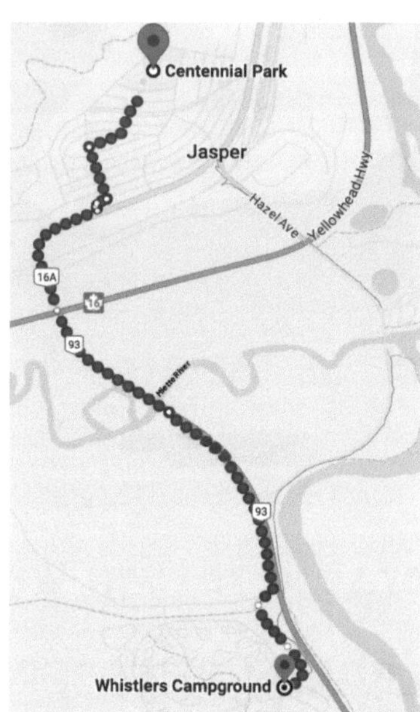

Horseshoe Lake, Jasper, AB, 2011. This was the photo taken on Canada Day, used for the lost dog posters placed around town, and later printed in the Jasper Fitzhugh newspaper.	A map showing Jasper's great escape from Centennial Park, across the Miette River, to Whistlers Campground.	Jasper and Amanda hiking the following years in Jasper, AB. Valley of the Five Lakes, 2012. Snaring River, 2013.

About the Author ~

Amanda Skwarok is a dedicated therapist specializing in children's and teens' mental health. As a former elementary teacher, she is passionate about literature and finds inspiration through reading and spending time outdoors, often accompanied by her loyal canine companions. Whether hiking in the mountains or exploring new trails, her love for nature and animals continually fuels her creativity and commitment to helping others.

Amanda's deep connection to nature was shaped by countless family vacations to Jasper National Park during her childhood. Jasper's breathtaking landscapes and the warmth of its community have left a lasting impression on her and deeply inspired her work.

In this book, Amanda aims to raise awareness of the importance of keeping pets safe during potentially stressful events like fireworks. She highlights that loud noises can be dangerous for reactive or non-desensitized pets and advocates for using a harness rather than a collar, or better yet, keeping pets indoors when possible.

Acknowledgement

This book is not just a story but a tribute to Jasper, Alberta.
Jasper holds a special place in the hearts of many, from its stunning
panoramic views to the welcoming spirit of its community.

This year, Jasper and its surrounding areas have faced significant
challenges due to devastating wildfires. These fires have impacted
both the natural beauty of the region and the lives of its residents.
As a small token of appreciation and support, I am pledging a
portion of the royalties from the sale of this book to the
Jasper Fire Caring Community Fund.

By purchasing this book, you're not only enjoying a heartfelt story
but also contributing to the recovery and restoration efforts in Jasper.
Together, we can help preserve the beauty and spirit of this
extraordinary place for generations to come.

Thank you for being part of this journey.
~